DEDICATED TO THE
RAVERS, MOVERS AND
SHAKERS (DJs, MCs,
PRODUCERS, ARTISTS,
LABELS, PROMOTERS,
DANCERS, RADIO STATIONS,
RECORD SHOPS)
FOR MAKING THE SCENE
AND MEMORIES
SO SPECIAL.

is for Ayia Napa

The place to be every summer to experience UK Garage in its fullest, from Anthill Mob to Artful Dodger to Agent X. House had Ibiza and UK Garage had "Ayia Napa! Ayia Napa! Ayia Napa!"

B

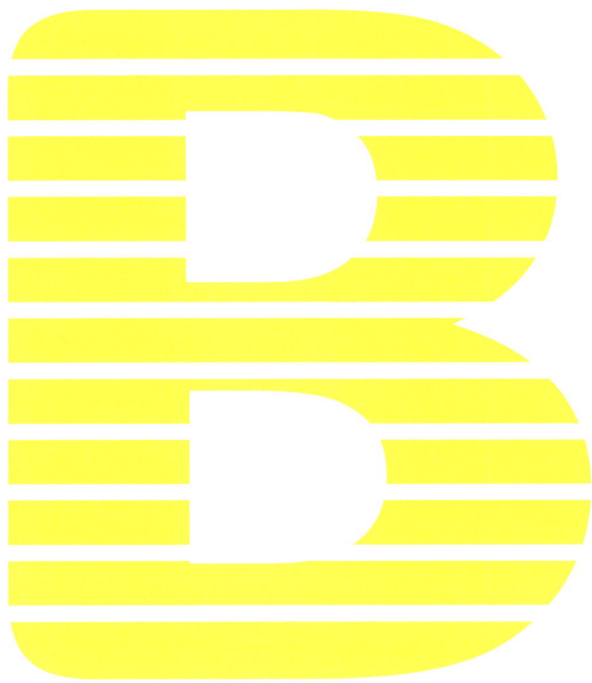

is for Boooooo!

There were horns, there were whistles, there was the shout Bo! and then came Boooooo! At some point, you'd hear this ringing out over raves whenever there was a rewind or a tune dropped. You might have been bubbling to a Brasstooth or Booker T tune at Bagley's with Mr Blakey on the mic and this is what you'd shout to show your appreciation. Perplexing initially, it became infectious with even people outside Garage saying it and then came that banger by Sticky and Ms. Dynamite and the saying was officially sealed *Booo!*

C

**is for the
Conductor Dance**

MAKE THE BODY
MOVE YOU GOT
TO LET THE BODY
GROOVE

The dance that became synonymous with Garage. From Camden Palace to Club Colosseum, you'd see guys and girls alike with index fingers waving conductor style (see Architechs *Body Groove* video). If fingers were freed up from holding champs (champagne), horns or whistles, they were doing this dance. Credit to MC CKP who supposedly started it.

D

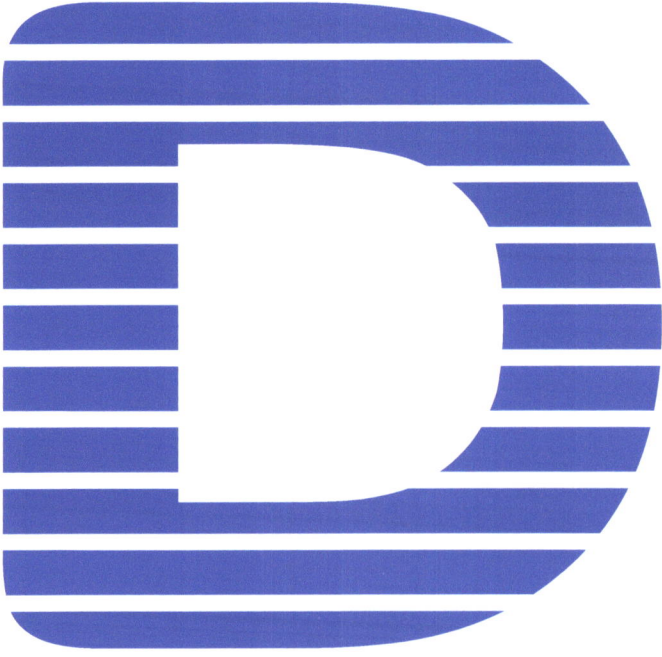

is for
the Dreem Teem

TIMMI MAGIC
MIKEE B
DJ SPOONY

Timmi Magic, Mikee B and DJ Spoony with shows on Kiss FM followed by Radio 1, compilations, big remixes like *My Desire* by Amira, Neneh Cherry's *Buddy X* and *Tears* by Underground Solution featuring Colour Girl and that unforgettable 1997 tune *The Theme* aka "eh eh, oh oh oh. She told me it's a..."

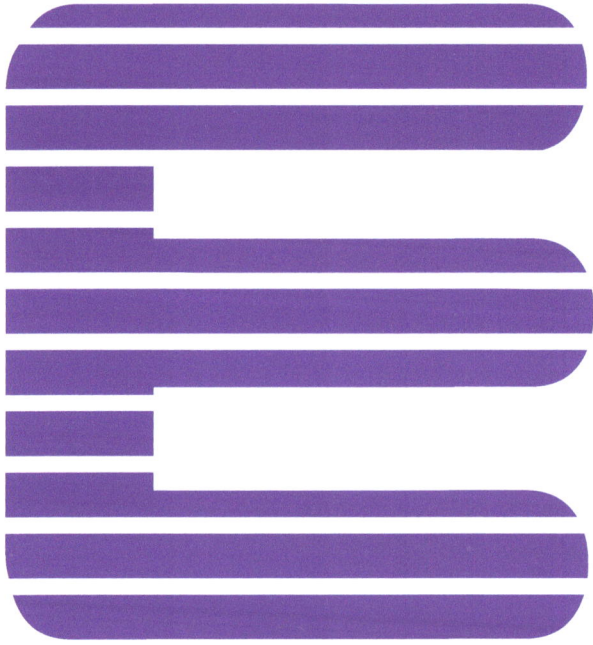

is for EZ

DJ EZ's style of quick mixing, dropping tunes and cutting in and out of tracks would make crowds go absolutely hyper. His intros brought excitement whether you were at Exposure or Experience, hearing "DJ DJ. EZ EZ" you knew what was coming.

is for Freek FM

Freek'N'You

End of Summer Party

Saturday 12th September '98
@ The Camden Palace
1a Camden High St NW1
10pm - 7am

Main Room
CHUCKIE • SNOOP
BLUE • JAZZY-D B2B BULLET
MIKE "RUFF CUT" LLOYD
RAMSEY & FEN • JASON-K
EZ "VOTED BEST DJ 1998"
SPECIAL-K • FEMMIE-B
LIVE P.A. "ICE CREAM RECORDS"
MC'S
CREED • C-K-P • BLAKEY • DT

Room Two
RANDOM • EASY-E
ECCO B2B JOHNNY 2 BAD
EASY RIDER • LEWI

BUBBLINGCREW
"ROJA, YANKEE, MYSTIC MATT"
LAVAL • RUSHIED
JOHNNY-J B2B BAZZA (RT CREW)
LIVE BONGO'S
MC'S
DOLLARS • FLAVA • 2 TON

FREEK'N' YOU "End of summer Party"
STAY LOCKED TO FREEK 101.8FM

UK Garage's leading pirate radio station based in North London and 101.8FM on the dial that was home to a number of DJs and MCs at some point including DJ EZ and Timmi Magic. If you tuned in, you might have got some *Flowers* or *FlyBi* but you would've definitely got some Four to the Floor (4x4).

is for Grant Nelson

The man behind Bump & Flex (massive remix of Indo's *R U Sleeping*), N'n'G (with Norris Da Boss Windross *Right Before My Eyes*) and 24Hour Experience with that absolute classic *Together* ("Don't Need It, Don't Want It, Don't Need It"). Club nights from Gass Club to Garage Nation, you were guaranteed to hear a Bump & Flex remix.

Another G is Groove Chronicles, consisting of El-B and Noodles, whose productions you also wouldn't hear a DJ set without like "Ma-Ma-Masterplaaan" (*Masterplan*), the Myron *We Can Get Down* remix to name just a few and the track of 99, *1999*.

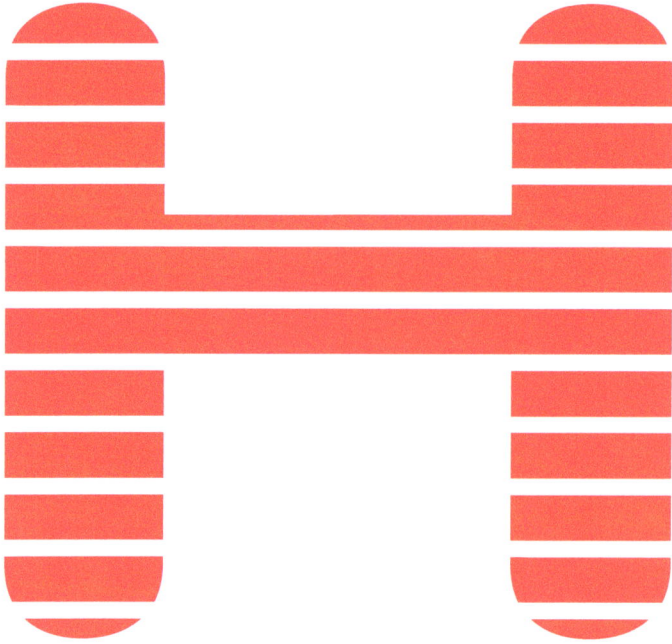

is for
House & Garage

Before it was UKG or UK Garage, it was House & Garage. 'House & G' encompassed 2-step, 'Speed Garage' (a term better left on old compilations) and good old 4x4 played alongside US House cuts in raves. However...

H is also for Heartless Crew. It's only right to mention the lively North London crew with DJ Fonti and MCs Bushkin and Mighty Moe. Mixing RnB, Hip Hop and "Bashment Bashment Bashment Bash-ment" with Garage, delivering witty rhymes—female skankers, "if you want a reload you better explode"—they brought entertainment, they brought energy, they brought the vibe yo!

is for Iceberg

ICEBERG

since 1974

If there was one thing about the Garage scene, it was that ravers and labels went hand in hand. Not meaning record labels like the legendary Ice Cream Records but designer labels; crazy Mosch (Moschino), Versace, D&G, Patrick Cox, Iceberg. Iceberg with its jeans, shirts, t-shirts and jumpers for guys adorned with Sylvester the Cat, Mickey Mouse or other cartoon characters and for girls, its denim skirts; this made up the dress code. As did any label selling at Proibito in London's West End or simply Morgan or Kookai for ladies. Remember—smart, no caps or trainers.

J

**is for
Jacquart Brut
Mosaïque
Champagne**

What? You ask. Let's be honest how many people really checked for the brand they were drinking unless they were really pulling out the stops (but M for Moët and V for Veuve Clicquot are taken). It didn't matter, champagne was the drink to bubble with in a rave. Pay As U Go didn't have *Champagne Dance* and MC Champagne Bubblee didn't have that name for no reason! If your pounds didn't stretch that far though, you might have had a brandy and coke, Bacardi Breezer, Smirnoff Ice or Sambuca if you wanted to relive Napa.

Drinks aside, one unquestionable name in Garage is Jason Kaye. One of the original DJs at Garage Nation, part of Ordinary People (*The Message*) and owner of Social Circles label behind all those Sticky tunes including *Booo!*

K

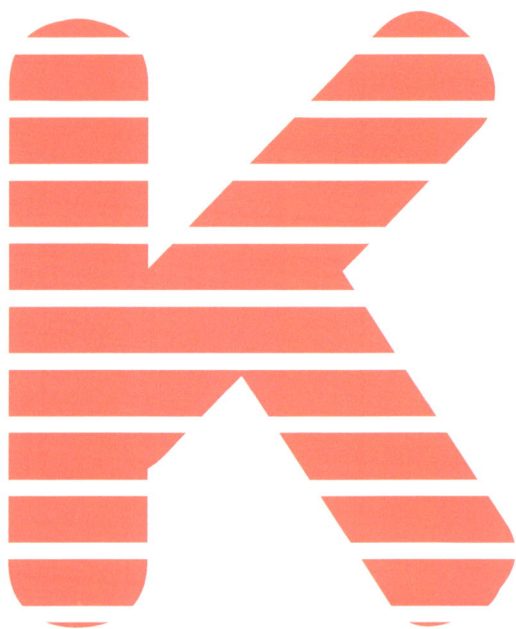

is for
Karl Tuff Enuff Brown

tuff jam

K is for Kele Le Roc whose *My Love (10° Below remix)* is a well loved anthem. K is for "Kinder Surprise" as MC Kie got ravers singing. K is for Kiss FM where Steve Jackson played UKG to the mainstream in the 90s. But K is also for Karl Tuff Enuff Brown. One half of Tuff Jam, along with Matt Jam Lamont, they also had a show on Kiss FM, brought back to back tunes on their Tuff Jam compilations, countless remixes like *Love Shy* by Kristine Blond and classics like *Key Dub*, *Just Can't Get Enough* under the moniker Caution, *Tumblin Down* and *Just Gets Better* (these last 3 featuring Xavier) all tunes to this day that just get better with "tiiiiime".

L

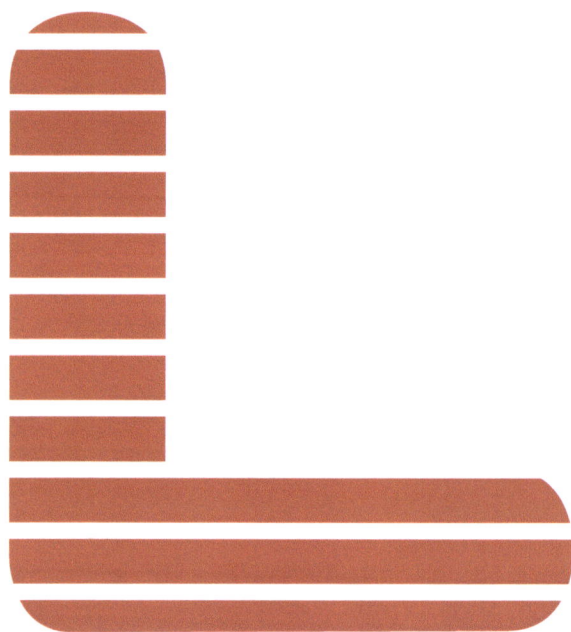

is for
La Cosa Nostra

There were a number of Garage promotions and La Cosa Nostra (LCN) was one of the big ones. It brought quality line ups and tape packs and gave many DJs, MCs and dancers a chance to shine and ravers good raves!

Old skool heads might also remember Lords of the Underground, Martin Larner's Liberty at Club Colosseum and Leisure Lounge in Holborn for Cookies & Cream and Cream of Da Crop.

is for MC

Holla wi di rinsin sound (MC Neat)

Pina Colada Ice Cream Shaker (MC CKP)

Stop DJ tell me what's gwaaning! (MC Blakey)

We're d-d-d-d-Doin it again (MC Creed)

Feel it coming in coming on (MC Ranking)

Rollin with the S the P the A the R the K the S (MC Sparks (RIP))

Uh bah bah Uh bah Uh bah bah Bad boy style (MC PSG)

Better get a move on, better get down (MC Charlie Brown (RIP))

Lovin it lovin it lovin it We're lovin it like that (MC DT)

How you like my How you like my How you like my styyyyle (MC Melody)

K Kinder Surprise I Into your eyes E Realise (MC Kie)

Here I go watch me flow how you mean! (MC Unknown)

When you hear 'du du duh' i'm coming (MC Sharky P)

Su-u-le-ec-ta (MC Viper)

Master of ceremonies. What would UKG be without the MCs. Memorable rhymes sitting nicely on tunes like Masterstepz's *Melody* and mixes by DJs like Mike Ruff Cut Lloyd. It all started with MC Creed and like Jungle before it, MCs would have you singing along and saying their lyrics in your everyday lingo, some songs just wouldn't be the same once you heard an MC over them and some things would become sayings beyond UKG and number 1 hits.

N

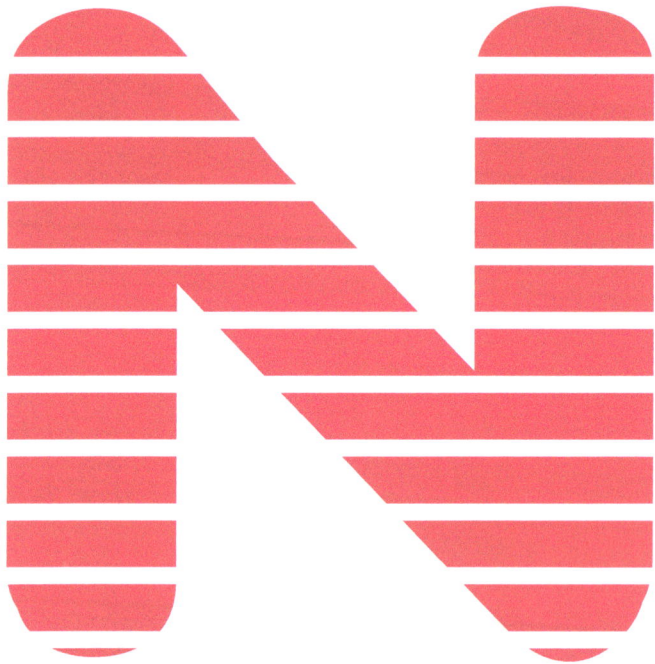

is for
'Never Gonna
Let You Go'

For many, this was the first 2-step track. The Kelly G remix of this US track by Tina Moore paved the way to the House & G we came to know and love. It was and still is a tune.

Noteworthy tunes like this were played by noteworthy DJs like Norris Da Boss Windross. He is one half of Pseudo and N'n'G with Grant Nelson and the driving force behind the UKG Awards, from which Garage became commonly known as UK Garage and UKG.

is for
"Oli Oli Oli!
Oi Oi Oi!"

The term that has transcended beyond Garage and become a well used chant to get the crowd going at any UK event. Did you know it was started by MC CKP shouting out his mate Oli?

is for
Pay As U Go Cartel

PAY AS U GO

"Know we, dem nuh know we". God's Gift, Major Ace (RIP), Maxwell D, Flowdan, Plague, DJ Slimzee, Geeneus, DJ Target and Wiley (who was also behind Phaze One *Nicole's Groove*, which must have played in every DJ's set in 2001) made up Pay As U Go out of East London's Rinse FM. Out of this super crew, Rinse FM, created by Slimzee and Geeneus, would become London's leading underground music station, Geeneus would help spear UK Funky but most notably, out of Pay As U Go Cartel we would see the creation of Grime, for which Wiley would quite rightly go on to receive an MBE.

is for
Quality
by Kym Mazelle
(RAFMAT Mix)

RAMSEY AND FEN
LOVE BUG LONDON
UNDERGROUND FM
MJ COLE SINCERE
RAFMAT

Two heavyweight production acts on one of their quintessential collaborations. Ramsey & Fen, who were on Freek FM and set up London Underground FM, brought UKG anthems like *Love Bug*, the remix of *Oh Boy* by Fabulous Baker Boys and the *Belo Horizonti* remix ("ah ohhhhh eh-eh"). MJ Cole brought another level of musicianship to 2-step with those bouncy jazzy chords on tracks like *Sincere* and remixes like *I Need Your Love* by Dub Syndicate Productions and Glamma Kid's *Taboo* featuring Shola Ama. They are just two examples of a number of quality producers who made Garage what it was and deserve their own pages.

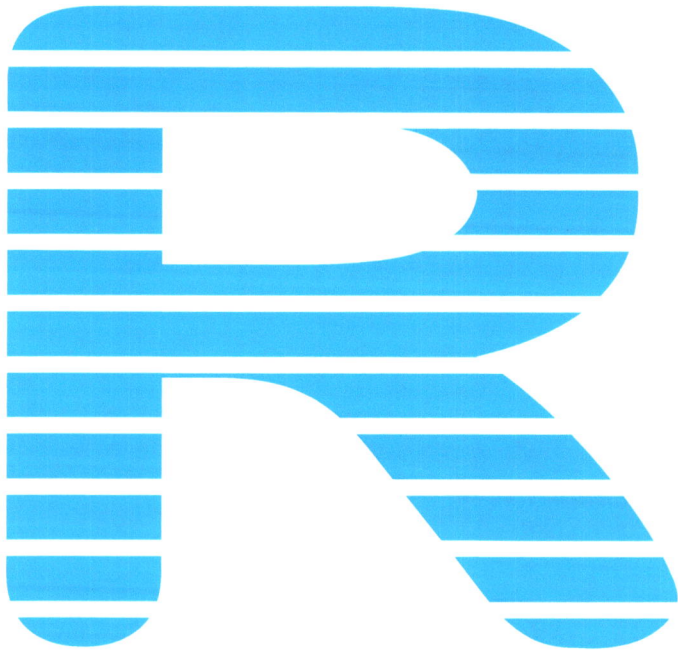

is for Raver

What was the scene without ravers! Roadblocks, rammed raves, queuing and R.O.A.R (God forbid the bouncer turning you away). Guys in shirts, suits, loafers. Girls in dresses and high heels. Bubbling away to Richie Dan on *R U Ready* wanting a reload or rrrrrewind. Champagne bottles, horns and whistles on the ready. Buying tickets from record shops, receiving flyers in the post, memberships, checking Channel 5 teletext page 345 for the latest raves. Raving was a thing from Sunday to Saturday.

is for So Solid

When *21 seconds* went to number 1 with its slick music video, it was a big moment for Garage and the UK music scene as a whole. Before this, South London was blessed with Delight FM, and the Garage Delight raves were held by the crew Megaman, Lisa Maffia, Asher D, Harvey, Romeo, G-Man, Swiss, "bound for the bound bound for the reload" Oxide & Neutrino plus more. These guys also put out underground favourites like *Dilemma*, *Woah* and of course "Oh no that's the word! Oh no that's the word!".

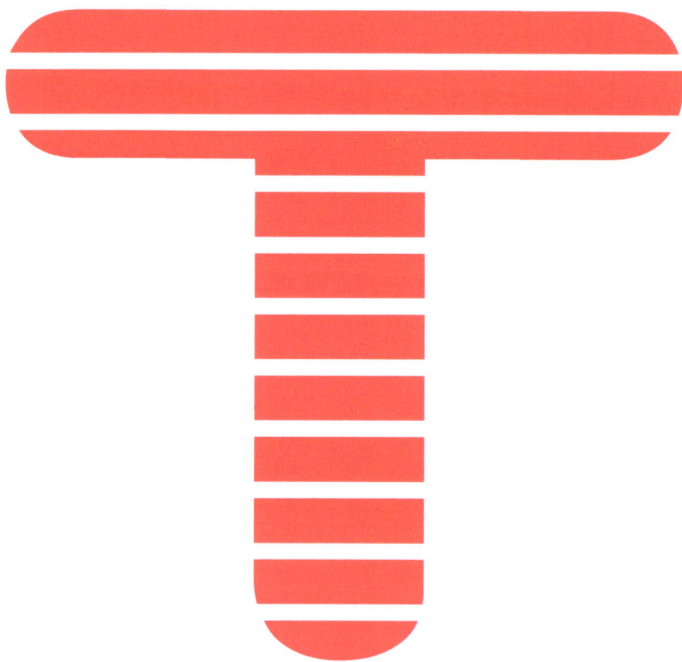

is for Tape Pack

GARAGE NATION
The Millennium celebration
MIKE 'RUFF CUT' LLOYD
Side A
DAT Recorded
All rights of the manufacturer and owner of the recorded works reserved. Unauthorised public performance, broadcasting and copying prohibited

GARAGE NATION
The Millennium celebration
E-Z
Side A
DAT Recorded
All rights of the manufacturer and owner of the recorded works reserved. Unauthorised public performance, broadcasting and copying prohibited

GARAGE NATION
The Millennium celebration
MARTIN LARNER
Side A
DAT Recorded
All rights of the manufacturer and owner of the recorded works reserved. Unauthorised public performance, broadcasting and copying prohibited

GARAGE NATION
The Millennium celebration
MIKEE B
Side A
DAT Recorded
All rights of the manufacturer and owner of the recorded works reserved. Unauthorised public performance, broadcasting and copying prohibited

GARAGE NATION
The Millennium celebration
PIED PIPER
Side A
DAT Recorded
All rights of the manufacturer and owner of the recorded works reserved. Unauthorised public performance, broadcasting and copying prohibited

GARAGE NATION
The Millennium celebration
NORRIS 'DA BOSS' WINDROSS
Side A
DAT Recorded
All rights of the manufacturer and owner of the recorded works reserved. Unauthorised public performance, broadcasting and copying prohibited

GARAGE NATION
The Millennium celebration
RAY HURLEY
Side A
DAT Recorded
All rights of the manufacturer and owner of the recorded works reserved. Unauthorised public performance, broadcasting and copying prohibited

GARAGE NATION
The Millennium celebration
JASON KAYE
Side A
DAT Recorded
All rights of the manufacturer and owner of the recorded works reserved. Unauthorised public performance, broadcasting and copying prohibited

Couldn't make the rave? Get the tape pack! 8 hours of glorious mixes with all your favourite DJs and MCs at Garage Nation, La Cosa Nostra, Exposure, Sun City, Stush, you name it. This is where you'd hear new tunes drop, ridiculous mixes, those catchy MC lyrics and if you had an EZ tape you would have been sure to get some Todd Edwards. The New Jersey, US producer is a must mention. Who didn't love a Todd beat with shuffling kicks and snares, samples and those distinct choppy vocals. *Push The Love*, *Never Far From You* and his remix of Sound of One's *As I Am* are just some classics.

is for Underground

Outside of tracks being on Top of the Pops and of course the number 1s, UK Garage was underground. Like hidden treasure, if you were messing about with the dial on your radio, amidst some crackling you'd have the pleasure of finding a golden 2-step beat that might dip each time the DJ would talk (and would have your tape deck ready to record). 'Underground House & Garage' would play on pirate radio stations like Upfront 99.3 FM and many others that helped spread the sound across the capital and nation.

is for Vinyl

White label promos, dubplates, all the releases came out on vinyl and many underground tunes remain on vinyl. DJs would get the latest tracks on vinyl and you'd hear it on radio, at raves, on tapes or you'd also buy the record if you didn't mess about. As Garage surfaced from the underground, we saw more CDs—compilations and singles but the record shop was the beginning of tunes circulating. Sadly many of the key record shops are no longer with us but though gone, they are not forgotten.

W

is for Wookie

Wookie

featuring Lain./**Battle**

A1 Battle (Full mix)
B1 Battle (M.J. Cole mix)
B2 Battle (Dobie mix part 1)
Cut: 13/06/2000

Wookie's remixes (Gabrielle's *Sunshine*, Sia's *Little Man*) and Wookie's tunes (*Down On Me*, *Scrappy*, *What's Going On*, *Battle* featuring Lain) became club bangers responsible for any good DJ set at the turn of the millennium and onwards. Tunes like *Storm* and *VCF* were bassline heavy, perfect for back to back MCing while tunes like *Battle* and *Back Up Back Up Back Up* brought a musical element. Whichever it was, it never disappointed. Hearing that steel drum sound melody followed by "little man" (yes that is what Sia's saying) would often result in a rewind.

is for XL Recordings

ARTFUL DODGER. ZED BIAS. MONSTA BOY
NU-BIRTH. DEM 2. ANTONIO.
ROY DAVIS JR. LOCKED ON

This label, now known for Adele, released one of Garage's biggest tunes at the start of the old skool era—Roy Davis Jr. featuring Peven Everett *Gabriel*. It was also parent label to Locked On, which released a ton of Garage anthems such as Nu-Birth's *Anytime*, Dem 2's *Destiny*, Somore's *I Refuse*, Doolally's *Straight From The Heart*, Antonio's *Hyperfunk*, Artful Dodger's *Movin Too Fast*, Zed Bias' *Neighbourhood*, Monsta Boy's *Sorry* featuring Denzie... Name that tune.

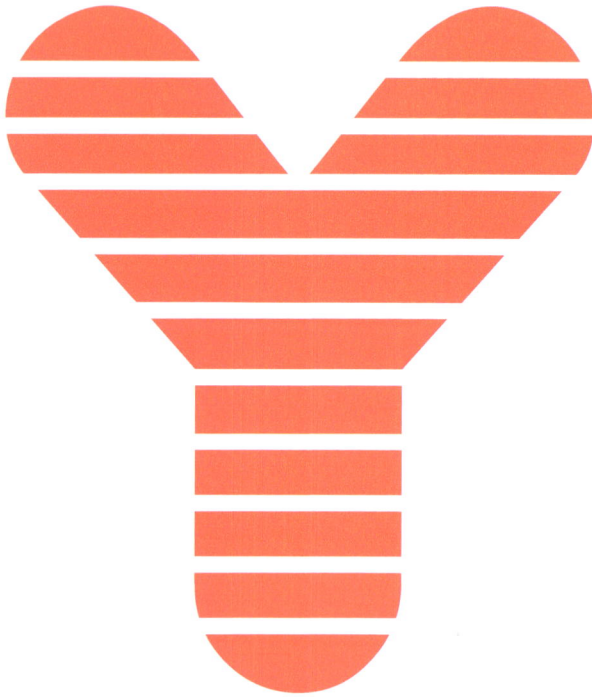

is for Y-Tribe

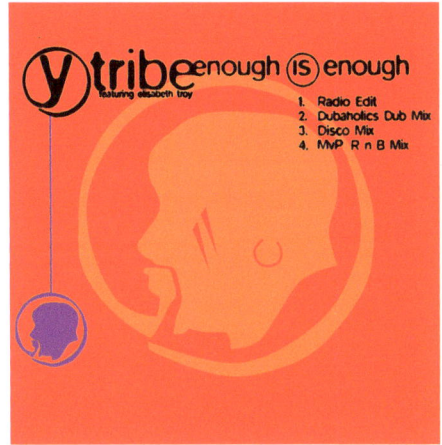

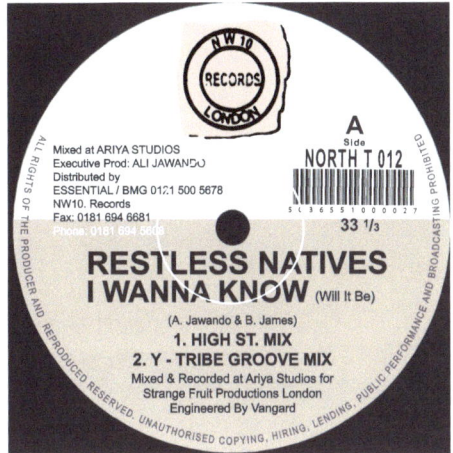

There were a number of sing-along tracks in Garage. TJ Cases' *You Bring Me Joy* is one example, a gem that brings nostalgia for many just as Garage brought many of us joy and Y-Tribe were behind some of the sing-along favourites. "Ba-by. You bring me up when I'm down" was straight catchy. *Enough is Enough* featuring Elisabeth Troy with that instantly recognisable classical intro and Colour Girl's *Joyrider* were big tunes that still have you singing along to this day. Y-Tribe were also behind *I Wanna Know* under the name Restless Natives again with an opening line you'd easily hear being sung in unison when the tune would drop—"I wake up 7:30, I've got things to do…"

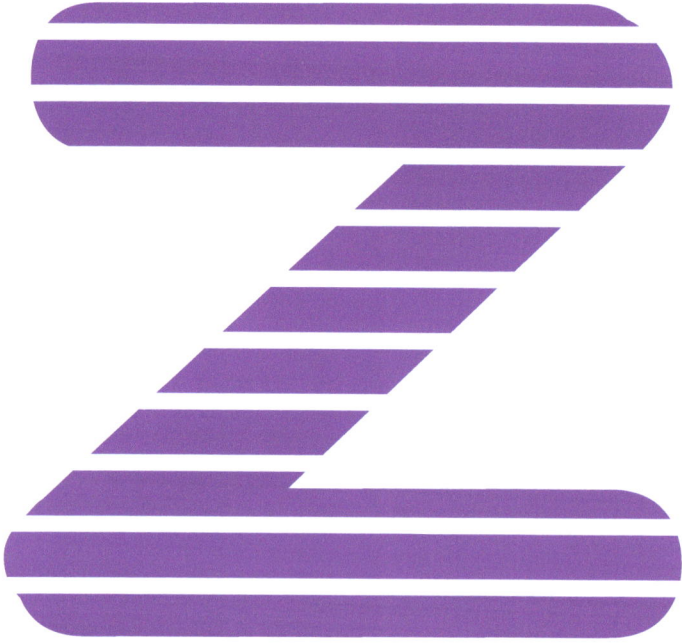

is for Zed Bias

"I feel good good good". What else can we say! Zed Bias' zingy productions and basslines like *Neighbourhood*, *Been Here Before* and his remix of E.S. Dubs' *Standard Hoodlum Issue* "reflex action, like a snake, like a snake...". Tunes!

www.ingramcontent.com/pod-product-compliance
Lightning Source LLC
Chambersburg PA
CBHW041957090426
42811CB00014B/1527